THE
NATURE YEAR
MAY

Safety note

Be safe whenever you are looking at nature or carrying out
activities. If you go for a walk in the countryside or park,
always take an adult with you and never wander off on your
own. Remember some wild animals and plants can be
dangerous: never eat any plants or fungi unless you are
certain what they are and watch out for animals and insects
with a venomous bite or sting. Never touch sharp objects
such as needles or broken glass. Always wash your hands
after touching natural materials.

The publishers have made every effort to ensure that the
activities in this book are safe and accurate. All activities
should be carried out under adult supervision. The
publishers cannot accept liability for any injury or damage
sustained while performing the activities.

First published in 2012 by Orpheus Books Ltd,
6 Church Green, Witney, Oxon OX28 4AW England
www.orpheusbooks.com

Created and produced by Nicholas Harris, Sarah Hartley, Katie Sexton,
Ruth Symons and Erica Williams, Orpheus Books Ltd.

Text by Ruth Symons

Scientific consultant Chris Jarvis, Oxford University Museum of
Natural History

Illustrated by Martin Camm and Ian Jackson

ISBN 978 1 905473 69 4

Printed and bound in Singapore

THE
NATURE YEAR

MAY

🎜 Orpheus

CONTENTS

THE WORLD
IN MAY

I N THE NORTHERN hemisphere, spring moves into summer. Most animals are breeding or raising their young by now. Meanwhile, in the southern hemisphere, winter is approaching. Some animals start to migrate to warmer lands to avoid winter altogether.

In the northern hemisphere, most migrant birds have arrived from their wintering grounds in the south. Many birds are building their nests, or gathering food for their newly-hatched chicks. Some early fledglings have already flown the nest.

By May, the martins have returned to Europe from Africa. Towards the end of the month, they find mates and start to build nests from mud and saliva. Martins usually fix their nests to the underside of cliff overhangs or under the eaves of buildings in towns and villages.

Most mammals stay with their young to protect them, or else leave them hidden from sight. In the forests of North America, Europe and Asia, many young are born with markings to camouflage them. For example, wild boars *(right)* are born with stripy fur to help them blend in with their woodland habitat.

A wild boar family forages for food on the forest floor.

In the southern hemisphere, the nights are growing longer and temperatures are starting to drop. In parts of South America and southern Africa, autumn marks the start of the rainy season. Around the continent of Antarctica, temperatures plummet and sea ice starts to form.

ARCTIC

AS TEMPERATURES RISE in the Arctic, the ice cap starts to melt and the sea ice breaks up. Polar bears follow the receding ice in pursuit of their main prey: seals. They may swim long distances between ice floes, but though the bears are strong swimmers, they cannot match a seal for speed in the water.

When the sea ice melts completely in the summer, bears either head further north, where the ice never melts, or swim to land until the sea freezes again in the autumn.

IN MAY, huge flocks of Arctic terns fly north to breed. They have flown all the way from Antarctica, a journey of nearly 35,000 kilometres. But this epic flight is worth the effort: by migrating, the terns can avoid the hardships of winter at either pole.

A pair of terns mob an Arctic fox.

The terns gather in large colonies to mate and breed. Their chicks would make an easy meal for a fox or gull, so the colony guards them fiercely. If a predator approaches, the birds assemble in an angry mob, squawking loudly and diving at the intruder's head with their sharp beaks.

EUROPE

AS THE SUN RISES, a roe deer leaves her fawn in the undergrowth at the edge of a forest. Until it is strong enough to run away from danger, the young deer is safest hidden from sight. The mother's presence will only attract the attention of predators, so she stays away for most of the day.

Fawns are born with spotty markings, to camouflage them in the dappled light of the forest floor. A fawn can stay perfectly still and silent for hours at a time. Any movement would give away its location and potentially attract danger.

A cherry tree in blossom

Meanwhile, across Europe, fruit trees burst into blossom *(above)*. The branches become busy with bees and other insects collecting pollen. When wind shakes the trees, petals cascade from the branches, covering the ground below.

EUROPE

O N THE BANKS of a river, May brings a flurry of activity. A family of mallard ducklings follow their mother across the water, while a kingfisher dives for fish. Her young family, concealed in the sandy riverbank, are constantly hungry.

At the water's edge, two brightly-coloured damselflies are clasped in a mating embrace. After a mid-air chase, the male grabs the female by the head and brings her to land on a water plant.

Close by, a mayfly prepares to take flight. Mayflies spend a year or more as nymphs before they leave the water and take their adult form. But their adult life lasts only one day. This is because they cannot feed; their only goal is to mate and lay eggs before they die.

NORTH AMERICA

ON THE GREAT LAKES, huge colonies of western grebes gather to breed. They have spent winter in the south, but fly north in spring to establish breeding colonies.

Before they mate, the grebes take part in elaborate courtship dances. Couples appear to trot across the water side by side, with their wings held back and their elegant necks curved upwards.

Once a couple have performed their dance, they set about building a nest. Grebes build floating nests, anchored by weeds in the lake floor. They make them close together, forming a large raft where the eggs are safe from land predators. They are so safe, in fact, that parents may even leave their eggs unguarded while they feed.

NORTH AMERICA

AS SUMMER approaches, ladybird larvae, hatched in the spring, change into adults. But in the American Southwest, they make this change at just the time when aphids, their main food, are dwindling in the summer heat. So the ladybirds leave the hot lowlands and fly to cooler hills nearby where they will sleep through the hottest months.

I N SOUTHERN CANADA, warmer weather signals the start of the breeding season for red-sided garter snakes. The snakes have spent winter crowded in rock crevices sheltering from frosts, but now they start to emerge.

Males are the first to venture out. They crowd around cracks in the rock, waiting for females to stir. As each female comes out, she is quickly surrounded by males, all competing to mate with her. "Mating balls" of males around one female may contain up to 100 individuals.

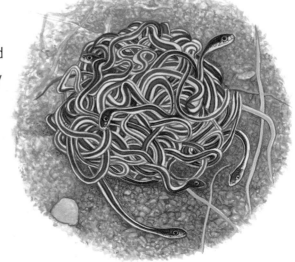

A mating ball of snakes writhes on the ground.

CENTRAL AMERICA

IN THE RAINFORESTS of western Costa Rica, heavy rains have drawn out a crowd of golden toads. Bright orange males gather around rainwater pools, waiting for females who come there to spawn. Males grab on to passing females and are carried to the pools. As the female releases her eggs into the water, the male fertilizes them.

*Two males
watch a female
in a pool after spawning.*

THE BREEDING SEASON for harpy eagles coincides with the start of the rainy season in April or May. Pairs build large nests high in the rainforest canopy. Both parents tend to the eggs, but after the first chick has hatched, all other eggs are abandoned. Chicks stay in the nest for about six months, dependent on food from their parents until they are forced to fend for themselves.

The harpy eagle is one of the largest birds of prey in the world. It is strong enough to carry away large prey, such as sloths and monkeys.

SOUTH ATLANTIC

ALONG THE BEACHES of Ascension Island, hundreds of green turtles are hatching. They are about to make the most dangerous journey of their lives: from their nests to the ocean.

The hatchlings scrape away the sand covering their nests then hurry towards the sea, guided by the sound of the surf. As they waddle across the beach, many of the young turtles are picked off by hungry gulls and crabs.

When they finally near the sea, the surviving turtles wait for a wave to carry them away. In the water they are safer. They can dodge the beaks of diving birds, but they must still avoid sharks. The young turtles search for rafts of floating seaweed. Here they can drift safely until they are big enough to swim in the open ocean.

SOUTHERN AFRICA

AMID THE SAVANNAH plains of southern Africa lie the swamplands of the Okavango Delta. The annual flooding, starting in May, draws a huge variety of animals to the region.

Buffalo, zebras and elephants flock to the area, but other animals live here all year round. Sitatunga antelopes live on the edge of the swamps, ducking under the water completely to hide from predators. Hippos spend their days in the water, coming out at night to feed on grass.

SOUTHERN AFRICA

AUTUMN IS THE MAIN mating season for the impala antelope. Males aim to establish a territory that will attract passing females, ideally an area of woodland, where the antelopes' young can be reared safely.

But most territories can only be won by defeating its owner in battle. Males lock horns and try to throw their opponents off balance. There may be so many challengers for a territory that the defending male has no time to eat. If this happens, he will grow so thin and weak that he is eventually overpowered.

While holding a territory is desirable, it also has its dangers. Impalas usually live in herds and alert each other to danger. A solitary male is more vulnerable to attack from predators, such as lions and cheetahs.

INDONESIA

INDONESIA'S DRY season brings long days of relentless sunshine and baking temperatures. The heat is making this tiger uncomfortable, so it looks for a place to cool down.

In the middle of a shaded valley, it finds a shallow pool. Approaching the water, the tiger drinks a little, then wades in up to its shoulders. It lies here submerged for an hour or two.

Tigers are the best swimmers of all the big cats. They even have slight webbing between their toes, which enables them to power through the water easily.

MAY IS THE START of the Komodo dragon's mating season. Males compete with each other over females and often fight to display their strength and dominance.

Fighting males grasp each other and stand on their hind legs, struggling to push over their rivals. Fights sometimes result in severe injury or even death.

THINGS TO DO:
MINI—BEAST FUNNEL

Mini-beasts include insects, spiders, worms, woodlice and other types of small creature. Try this activity to get a closer look at mini-beasts.

1 Wearing gardening gloves, scoop up some fallen leaves from the ground. The longer the leaves have been there, the more mini-beasts will have made their home amongst them.

2 Place a plastic funnel in the mouth of a glass jar. If you do not have a funnel, you can easily make one by rolling up a piece of card or paper.

3 Fill the funnel with the leaves you have gathered and place it beneath a lamp—not too close or your mini-beasts will overheat. Leave the funnel there for an hour or two.

4 The mini-beasts will avoid the heat and light of the lamp by wriggling downwards and dropping into the jar.

5 Now you can have a good look at the mini-beasts.

6 When you have finished looking at the mini-beasts, make sure you put them back where you found them.

THINGS TO DO:
DANDELION INVISIBLE INK

Pick a fresh-looking dandelion with a bright yellow flower head—that is, before it goes to seed and turns grey and fluffy.

Holding the dandelion like a pen, use the sap from its stalk to write a message or draw a picture on a piece of white paper.

You won't be able to see anything straight away. Leave the paper to dry and your message will gradually become visible!

NATURE WATCH

	Bluebells	*10*
	A fern uncurling	*20*
	A ladybird flying	*30*
	Broken eggshells	*40*
	A dragonfly	*50*

See how many of these things that typically happen in May you can spot. Award yourself the points on the right!